THE TRUE MEANING OF *Christmas*

The True Meaning of Christmas Is . . .

God Himself has come to us

"I bring you good tidings of great joy, which shall be to all people. For unto you is born this day in the city of David a Saviour, which is Christ the Lord."

Luke 2:10-11

God the Son has become man

"Christ Jesus, who, being in the form of God, thought it not robbery to be equal with God: But made himself of no reputation, and took upon him the form of a servant, and was made in the likeness of men: And being found in fashion as a man, he humbled himself, and became obedient unto death, even the death of the cross."

Philippians 2:5-8

God's most wonderful gift to us

"For God so loved the world, that he gave his only begotten Son, that whosoever believeth in him should not perish, but have everlasting life."

John 3:16

"For the wages of sin is death; but the gift of God is eternal life through Jesus Christ our Lord."

Romans 6:23

This Christmas you can experience the true meaning of Christmas—Jesus Christ—and receive forgiveness of sins, joy beyond measure, and eternal life with God in Heaven. Won't you receive Jesus Christ, the risen Son of God, as your personal Saviour?

"But as many as received him, to them gave he power to become the sons of God, even to them that believe on his name."

John 1:12

To read the Bible, learn about Jesus, or find a church in your area, visit **Crossway.org/LearnMore.**

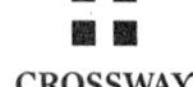

CROSSWAY

GOOD NEWS *Tracts*

www.goodnewstracts.org